It Can Take Till Now

Also by Elizabeth Goodsir
Wind Rippling Water (2015)
Blue Pollen Beautiful (2017)

Elizabeth Goodsir

It Can Take Till Now

It Can Take Till Now
ISBN 978 1 76041 704 8
Copyright © text Elizabeth Goodsir 2019
Copyright © images Bruce Goodsir 2019

First published 2019 by
GINNINDERRA PRESS
PO Box 3461 Port Adelaide 5015
www.ginninderrapress.com.au

hugs and blessings galore
to ten beloved
grandchildren

their visit is frail

In the silence

I listen to a lit candle
red poinsettia

breath moving
lips to prayer

to voice made by
the touch of hands

words formed by
raised print

thoughts landing
without sound

inside the silence
I hear

I watched a child today

and felt for his tiny heart
a young man flirted with his mother
their happiness was not the kind
that children are included in

Children simply feel what they feel

and know when they are not
the apple of someone's eye

Reunion

I had hoped our days together
as three long time friends
would be still, silent, smiling

sharing gently things we now know
but I was not ready to be quiet
needed to talk and challenge

wanted to push us to our edges
to the rocks and abysses
of our minds

look at the knotty and hard things
speak old words we can't retract
have their rocks match mine

they were here for
love and understanding
for ease and peace and pleasure

what was the urgency
the need to examine
to judge

I'm left remembering
knowing
is not always a battle

it comes with
quiet trust
faith in the unfolding

Kitchen wisdom

today I was reminded of silver rings
a ring of protection   a ring of compassion
rings of mindful generosity
more honest than mindless availability

around a table of caring sharing women
I learnt the art of dropping circles
loops that honour self
allow for other

there is beauty in tossing hoops
making lines around where we
begin and end
where others start and finish

delicate marks
that allow you
to be you
me to be me

Fare thee well

lightly as a wind-blown feather
you fluttered out of our bay side days
leaving the space between our houses
loud with that erupting laughter

and still I hear the songs
you sang bursting
through sea doors
lovelier than gulls' call

and such tiny feet pedaling
polished fingertips straddling the keys
clever breath blowing open music sheets
between such red singing lips

the sounds of wind chimes
you hung amongst rock ponds
and potted ferns
breeze in the cockatoo vane

the rich purr of your hatchback
returning to light the fire   feed the strays
curl up in time for the western
drama of kaleidoscope sky

the whisper of
unearned happiness
from your door
to mine

I have taken a risk

I am not passing my words by
holders of cultural standards

I want to leave them as they have arrived
they feel such mystery that land in

my fingertips and I tap them out
before they lift off again

their visit is frail
if I handle them they bruise and collapse

or become like polished fruit

You came with your

mountain look
and enkindled eyes

luring me from my poorly ways
to rise higher into possibility

now departed I'm learning
your expectation

and to be kind to
my dissatisfaction

I'm leaning into
a larger you

Selection

watching from the sideline
I was attached by osmosis
could feel him wondering
if he was not the kind of boy
the squad wanted to have

I was already
doubled-up
with rejection

but needed to show him
it didn't matter
he returned my thumbs up
and his smile released me

St Paul

There is a message about love
in a letter to the Corinthians

Love is patient, it is kind
it does not envy, it does not boast
it is not proud, does not dishonour others
it is not self-seeking, not easily angered
it keeps no record of wrongs
it always protects
always trusts
always hopes
always perseveres

but I ache for children living nightmares of abuse
of the chaos and contradiction
crippling fear

of the haughty and the proud and powerful
their scorn   their cankerous words
their untruth

by the sea I understand that love does not
falter in its task
it lives freely   exquisitely in its patience

and we must live in awe

Morning in Melbourne

beneath an air balloon
stilled in the sky
a wizened lady touched
her feet like a breath
of childhood
her smile perfect through
baby pink gums

In her peace

I listened to the silent trees
one bird sitting still
one leaf turning

the first rain drop
three circles in the pond
two falling blossoms

Our white house on the bay

is the sound of waves
and tree laughter

salty breeze
sways wild iris

a tanker slinks
satin river

leaving a slow
humpback wake

inside is still   gold
where we map our souls

did you hear that bird

Breathless

trees stapled to the dirt
their leaves stilled prayer flags
gum blossom pressed bridal petals

invisible air pauses
no sound from the sea
unsung crochets wait on black lines

only the clouds finger the earth
like potters
with their glazes

Through travail

and travel's long haul
you pulsed into my garden

dropped into the
bottle brush

opened your crimson throat
and we sang-in the morning

Such greetings

everywhere is a circle of song
a medley of love notes
bird welcome
waving through the sky
strings of gesture and grace
threading blue air

crimson clouds crowning
moments   monuments
orange sun slipping into
gold
falling   fading leaves
settling   new places

everywhere
knowing
how to be

There's a blue wren

and it teaches me
sing! sing!
till your breast swells

gather sticks and leaves
be patient with the wind
fluff open to the sun

bath in the dirt
squat in the rain
feel the air beating your life

Low cloud

cloaked the mountain
drifted across steely wavelets
and fell on the shoulders of a seagull

Tree

bare of leaves
hollowed
night cool
silver clean

bird home
moon frame
tomorrow's
dawn catcher

proof of
ancient silence
eternity of
the sun

in time
stone
star
stairway

For Prue

In the air is

seen and unseen
the silence of a note
birds without colour

words without language
weeping that's trapped
smiles that glow inside

there are the faint
sighs of death
and shapes of not-yet born

timeless pilgrims
reminding us to notice
nothing

hang in the air

Something tricked the birds

into morning
a treefull began singing in the night

I felt the unrest of your breath
and knew you were dying

the dawn stayed still
silver rain hung loosely

like the rippled roll of a shutter
my heart rose and fell to a close

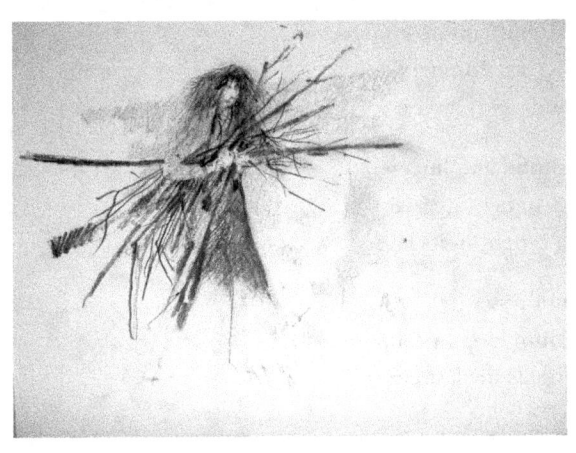

which is more beautiful

He gave her an onion

white rings in brown paper
its kiss stays on her lips
it blinds with its tears

its faithful and lingers
clings to her fingers
there is light in its layers

she undresses it
platinum loop by loop
and holds the last circle

to her heart

Dear Sheila

in a band of winter light you live
across shady water

I scour the wooded hill for the
terracotta tiles, white walls

decipher lit windows
from the pinpricked sky

imagine you head bent
intent or far gazing

hear you talking to the night
with the swish of a curtain

I feel your thoughts on
closing the book

the murmur of your lips
as you turn down the lamp

in the morning
your bedroom window

will be the first
the sun sets on fire

My pilgrim friend

each on retreat

at the Ganges you gathered to pay homage
chant and float lighted candles

we mustered with other campers
for summer by the sea

you practised yoga postures
quiet pondering poses

we were fishing   swimming
saluting the sun

both in baptism
both in gratitude

we praised and played
spilled joy – spread grace

in far away hemispheres
opposite seasons

we mirrored each other's peace
echoed each other's prayer

For Aurora

First touch

I wish I could remember that first day
you took my two hands in yours
greeting me to The Bay

so dull was I to see and foresee
I let it pass as warm and welcoming
unrecorded – its date slipped away

thank God there are days now to
notice every sweet thing you are
receive each new morning hand in hand

across the road we greet
at every chance
they're numbered now

what meant so little once
means so much
no need to speak

enough…just to gaze
promising
all is well

Night gifts

some women glow the house
my neighbour stands alone in her kitchen
opera soaring   chandeliers alight
dark-haired and clothed in red
fingering tiny crêpes she fills
trays with her cooking art

food is her voice her open arms
the smile behind her empty eyes
the offering for all she cannot do
she blends and folds and whips
her tears
spreads and layers her secret pain

she is a scarlet heart
warming the chill black night
with platters of stories and memories
of blessings and greetings and care

before the greedy cancer
takes its last horrible bite

Without you

I speak to you in the jutted blue
and hear you on the ridges of the wind

I can see you in the wintry tide
you are with me in the sharpness of the dark

I feel you in my dry-eyed tears
and in my brave   loud song

I whisper as the labouring night
delivers one more dusty ordinary day

Once

her body was a weapon
her eyes drowned capricious hearts
her shadow lured souls
till they yearned for themselves

old now
she peels fruit
of patience   gratitude
for no one   everyone

Soon

she kisses and wonders
which is more beautiful
the gazing before
or the velvet on his lips

he made her notice herself
so heartened
she left behind her
blinding shadow

Finale: a grandmother prompts a song

I think in the end
I want you to sing
something like this, she half-murmured

I will look for you
knowing you will follow

see you in the strong wind
holding each swallow

notice you in beating
sun or blowing rain

on up hill tracks
in life's dull pain

watch you in our children's swinging step
in their knowing words – defined and deft

in amongst loves and dreams
disappointments and boundless schemes

part of every secret that visits and lingers
beside each heart when life fumbles and fingers

I will feel your breath beside mine again
and no longer ask why   how   when

we followed her instruction and sing it to the tune
On Top of Old Smokey

She keeps their house

Florence glides
washing and wiping   defrosting   degreasing
placing her kindness in forgotten corners
finding new homes for abandoned hope and want

there's a kiss in each item of washing she folds
a song as she sweeps verandas and paths
a word to the chooks and ducks on her way
to water the vegies   gather kindling and cones

sifting and sorting without consent
she makes neat piles for others to solve
picking and packing and making more space
trusting its helpful not causing regret

pausing to breathe in the wonder of life
she sips tea from a cup of the family she loves
delights in a treat of baked sugar and fruit
shares the lull with puss on her lap

planning the meal
preparing and peeling
grating and chopping
saucing and glazing

everyone's favourite food
is known
each will delight in their
own Florentine

leaving the gate with a stride and a wish
she returns in the morning in time
for toast on a porcelain rose
tea in blue bone china

already a cat on her lap
Labrador head on her shoe
she bows her head to the mountain
to bless her waiting day

her hands impatient
for service
there is no stopping
this wall to wall heart

Diagnosis

at midday the rain came
navy-blue city
washed itself grey
gutters filled with rainbows

headlights and blurred windows
like hope in trickled memory

and I watched those father's hands
move to your eyes
to keep the bulging
grief in

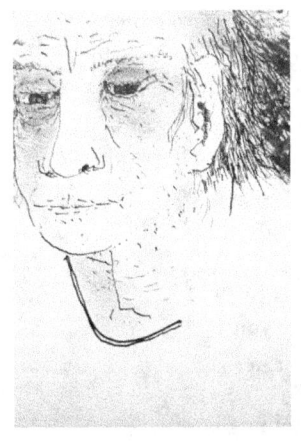

does it straighten at the ending

Baptism and marriage

I'll always wish you were always here
side by side on hot sand or alone whilst
I immerse myself in freezing water

chin on knees you scan the horizon
check once more that icy river
hasn't trapped me alive

I'm a bride again as I run
the shore watching you
open your windcheater

wrapping my trembling body
in your warmth your smell
your promise

the same two sea birds
waddle beside us
as we leave the sun blessed font

I dreamed of all that you are

how you tender touch
show anger
smile deep warmth
bare body of stone

eyes that tell or do not

your voice that disapproves
demands restraint
urges me on
gives me strength

speaks truths and warnings

that embrace of care
shrug of who cares
the compassion generosity
discipline and focus

arms of safety and promise

I dreamed the secrets
were all over
holding was gone
day was now blacker than night

I feared I hadn't caught all that you are

a hand moved across the sheets
resting quietly in mine
a new sun
showed me

you are more than I could ever dream

You

pondering the skyline
arms folded loosely behind
sandals landing on tide-washed sand
here comes my heart   I hear me say

How many

days have
we watched
climb a new start

how many
leaves have fallen
across our winters

how many swallows
have returned
with their mischief

how many moons
have we kissed
into darkness

how long will
our love
keep bending

does it straighten
at the
ending

Quoting

last night you wrestled with
frustration

saying others knew
how to catch letters

and make words that
you could never find

'your voice breaks like a flower
it trembles swaying on its taut stem

sounds turn to touch
making my eyes close'

you purred from your reading corner
wishing they were your own

you are my natural spring
your pulse my stillness

your voice licks
and balms my fire

I hear your caress
in every cell

I breathe because of
the beat of you

surely you can see
the beauty of your sound

I murmured

there are no shadows in his gaze

When your hand

touches mine
it is that love that passed
hand to hand
from way beyond
and the traces that it makes
are the same as the
fingers that light the
surface of the sea

Interlude with Barbara

today we stretched
a mosquito net
to keep out our
thoughts

fine enough to let in
the shimmers
of so much
tenderness

Acknowledgement and love to a co-writing co-grandmother

lizard and berry and wild pear

Beside the Finke River

a cold breath brushes rocks
ripples gold weed

setting sun tingles our coppery skin
kindles hatless hair

across the shifting sand
our yellow camper van

catches the last light of day
bouncing it in time

a streak of ochre in
the white river bed

We lived

under our
'flooded gum'

moonlight drenched
its ghostly crown

beside its trunk
we spent our days

in the understorey of
tar-hot rocks   sticks   river grit

we heard its vascular system
smelt its mix of black tea and tobacco

and waited for generations
to drift into its night shade

En route

we travel on long roads across
bare   smooth momentum

now and again shallow tracks
intersect nothing

an undulating line presses
against the horizon

rock and sand collapse
to form a basin

daring a corrugated track
we scratch our way amongst silver scrub

set up camp in wind rattled brush
clouds stack and stare

poised for the first
fat   wet   drops

Grandmother

tells me in her youth
she hunted fish
her body was a serpent
her eyes black spears

mid life she told stories
danced the moon into place
took kids back to country
dragged men from the drink

today she speaks of
caterpillar and emu
feeds on lizard, berry, wild pear
scarcely sings herself home

listen to the earth
and hear yourself

Desert mother

around her
dogs lick the silence

rosella feathers pant
lizards slow-slink

her smile turns gold
the spinifex grass

In Alice

we joined a group of women
cross-legged in the sun
stitching their
stories into felt

now I have a piece
of their Dreaming
on my chest
of drawers

Caterpillar hills

where wind climbs
and sand chases
stones scatter
ruby and jet

spikes of diamond
amber   topaz
towering bluffs of
deep-scarred purple

sudden gorges
of jubilant song
black trunks glued to
tourmaline sky

two crows drift
on rising ash
gliding our day
into scorched stillness

As if in a Christmas snow dome

flakes of silver and white shake across the sky
milky way a flurry leading the moon into the sky
like a team of bejewelled horses

a low slung Southern Cross spreads
and spirals the galaxy
pointer ever faithful to its task

we lie amongst fractures
made
nine hundred million years ago

it can take till now

Wall flower

you have played for time
beneath bitumen and black rock

curled tight through the moon sets
and weak winter dawns

until today when you turned
and pushed your face

towards October
and into my walking morning

Today there have been perfect things

magpies singing up the winter sun

dying friend lies lip to lip with her

six-week-old puppy

marching kayaks shake up a sleeping river

a builder whistles a heavy plank up the ladder

silver anniversary jug catches ancient sun drops

western sky bounces off golden floorboards

a white brie moon eats the shortest day

Beatified

motionless nectary gum blossom
stares at the sea
leaves weighted with stillness
offer their silence
branches hold themselves in awe
as the priest with the holy sacrifice

In the city

chimneys rise into the
tremulous night
grey and empty

a summer moon
drapes light on
street poles

marching
a white army
uphill

River gums

they could be dancers
as they curve   sway   breathe

sometimes a snarl of arrogance
a grown of pride

whisper of submission
elegance

their leaves touch
they make beauty

limbs sweep
bow   curtsey

anchored into
their dry river stage

they ready for night's
last curtain call

To Lee Lee

Bay of Possums

here in this beach shell life
ink stained hills and
mountain shapes

no crashing of waves
only the sound of water
curling like breaking an egg

sky and sea meet in summer blue
on a straight   strong line
that matches

the tall T-shirt
whitewashing
our new sea wall

Beach

warmth of the sun
draws eyelids
closed

presses us into
the heat
of the sand

sea beauty tingles
every pore   cell
each shining limb

hours fall like
summer fruit
round   pungent

For Beth

My own tube

syrup sky streaked rose crimson
purpled shore and indigo rocks
an onyx mountain its edges gilded
taffeta sea shot bronze   green   gold

straying clouds carrying honey
filigreed trees sequined and soldered
salt-filled breeze spinning foam and spray
flattened birds skid slippery slide air

no rotating
coloured glass
could reflect such
patterned wonder

When we had goats

grazing on new grass
their heads bent in gratitude

they'd panic when the sky changed
to lightning flash and puckered rain

raise their drawn skulls
and delicate hooves

to thunder down the hill
in a cloud of favourite dust

Spring fingers

whole fields
drowsy towns
sleeping bush

changes light
lengthens time
stretches space

turns up song
washes winter
into sun

The mountain

surfaces each day from
morning mist
lets it drop from its
shoulders
like something too tight

shows its form and shape
and hue for painters
to depict   defile
then clads itself again
in untapped glory and splendour

a volcanic feast of temptation

The wonder

of a candle flame
dissolving night

just a little so the
shadows can shine

Dusk from my garden chair

saucepan scraped at open window
dog insisting it be noticed
shuttlecock and family laughter
patient trumpet taught and tamed

six o'clock news disasters
washing machine tries to stop
forgotten oven smelling and smoking
someone's car will not start

once inside there will only be
the sound of silent   scarcely-lit me

I watched an elder today

she is brave and sassy and
has forgotten how to jump
no need to tip toe or frolic like lambs

she is steady with eyes that welcome and farewell
and a tail that bounces even when
most has been stolen

sometimes under a spell
she dreams of her winning wool
and sun wet grass

of being a cloud
that walks the sky
enlightened   eloquent   excited to be

she imagines looking down on her
anchored self
her stockinged   gloved   dignity

her ebony hooves
and pink damp nose
dainty in dawn-tipped clover

Evening in May

leafless limbs prick heavy sky
gardens curl in falling chill
rows of smoke hot lines to heaven
lights dulled in black-out drapes

doors close on profit or loss
snakes of cars blink and shirk
keys uncover emptiness
silence   togetherness

moon tugs the day from diaries
opens pages to fresh nothingness
trees know to stay in limbo
tomorrow's birds have no plans

This day

wrist   thumb   forefinger
closing   opening

bending   stretching
breathing   holding

postures   poses
resting   remembering

shafts of
circling light

morning greeting
complete

doors to sunshine
and music

tank water
tea packet

hairbrush and
sandal straps

white blouse
buttons of pearl

ocean swim
walk on sand

clothes pegs and
seed packets

seaweed mulch
green watering can

paper and ink
a birthday poem

folded eggs and parsley
candle on a scallop shell

such sweetness has
taken till noon

Then...

comes the dust
fine   grey
spreading dust

this dust you can't keep out
on your clothes
in your shoes

in your lungs   your nails
between your teeth
down your throat

it settles
around the heart
hardens

it settles like night
comes ready or not
you can't clean it up

hurry it up
can't retrieve from the dust
that last soft kiss

Returning

moody clouds
and melting mountains

sulking gums
and sunken tarns

patchwork food
gingerbread houses

we have crossed

the Strait

home

First light

morning stirs itself
from purple to pink gold

watery frills dance rocks
roll   scroll   return

first fisher smudges
a silky sea

white yacht butterflies
the cliff face

everywhere such
new day possibility

Awake

decrees flew like shuttlecocks
wreaking havoc in the heart

then light-footed and
full of song

children danced
tiny steps on tip toe

their fingers
scissoring the air

clipping the wings
of wayward words

did she notice

If

I were an ant
I'd guide each
shod foot till
it walked
on air

one sensible
sensitive
nine-year-old
advised
instructed

perhaps this is how
we learn sense

lift each other
with such kindness

nothing can be
trampled

All the things

I never said
hover and hurtle
circle   scream

in the darkness
in the silence

I panic and punish
play back   fast forward
imagine

and out of nowhere falling
into my own heart peace

I let your throat breathe
eye lids quiver
fingers tighten

and kiss the unspoken
into your waiting lips

The look

was learnt a long time ago
not that there had been hurt or unkindness

simply in having that baby her mother
had betrayed her

made her an outsider

Stroke

weighted to the shore
hinged to heavy legs
she watched the avid sea

tide rushed and dragged
white froth on fast blue
wind tossed a pale sun

licking the hot dry sand
from her crumpled hand
she ached to feel the deep wet salt

And I thought of

all the fists clenched in hostility
the faces wracked in battlefield pain
bodies stiff with blood and death

and I was thankful this stroke of misfortune
was not of hate   or blade   or bomb
wayward power   ruthless piety

it seemed to be as proof
of the possible and imperative
startling bravery and fragile truth

stoutly healing imbued tenderness
as I watched a young family
dip into love no curse or strike could subdue

Skin care

feet and hands scarred
and sun-roughened by day

in the thick darkness
tender as midnight silk

like kindness

we have to lose all we
hold and count and save
know desolate   sorrow-filled
landscape

to feel the delicate threads
of care and attention
deep inside
and waving from the crowd

touched by Naomi Shilhab Nye

Anzac Day

sun-scrubbed smile
peeling
half-toothed

spitting
voiceless
bravery

they stood ready
as in their
cold deep trenches

except now they inhabit
sunrise   soft windfall
drink pure stillness

listen without hearing
wait without waiting
watch light become dusk

stand to
and ask that we go
nowhere with guns

Beneath a sheet

I shake for the suffering
of a desperate heart

I have no words
no song to sing

or line to send
no change to make

any utterance
is old debris

no remedy
no certainty

a look   a judgement
with trails decades long

afraid to cause
regret or curse

rummaging or
expectation

my heart joins the stars
light years away

my song of nothing
part of heaven's roar

Reverence

he was the youngest son
in love with his mother
who could not resist her
youngest son's wonder

such bliss of growth
glory of action
splendour of beauty
life deliciously lived

to paint such a union
I'd wrap them in a silken cloak
blonde light trailing
and sudden shadows
eyes of leaf-green
and faces close and unmoving
never ceasing to be

Did she?

turn somersaults and Catherine wheels
sing in the garden as she peered into flowers
collect blue feathers dropped by the early wren

was she busy listening to the music in the leaves
gazing at landing butterflies

did she notice the sap from the peppermint tree
was that her drawing of the moon
chalky on black paper

did she tire playing alone with her dollies

did anyone know the name of her
make-believe friend
or why she arranged her books that way

did she weep when she'd been naughty
scold herself in her upstairs bedroom
wish that she'd been nicer to someone who hurt

did she giggle and scheme   tell stories and dream
share secrets with her sister   call her in the night
did they swap treasure   hide lollies for later

did she tumble and flop over outstretched parents
swing between held hands
let them catch her when she jumped

did she notice how loved she was
that there was no need to be shy
people were just waiting for her rose-tipped smile

or was she just wondering
what she might become
promising to be that with everything she was

may she have noticed her own fast growing
loving each life piece she'd put into place
even if it happened without her knowing

may she walk touched by her grace

Old habits

side by side
head to foot
ruffled feathers
wings alike

necks strained
ear to ear
tails touching
but never eyes

pigeon pair
promised
prepared
willing now
to be plucked

…dying hard

If I were a poet I'd be made of wood

quietly being essence
speaking strength
beauty   integrity

stripped bare

now at last in step

Sisters may be women who grew up under the same roof
or they may be dear friends
soul kin you meet on the way

sisterhood may mean having a friend who was there from the beginning   someone who can share childhood memories that nobody else can connect with in quite the same way

that sister can drive you crazy
or totally inspire you

no matter the shape or colour of life
the story or the imagining
the truth is a sister is irreplaceable

my sister and I lost something precious
from the beginning   we grew up in the same family   had the same story

lived side by side in the same intact unit of four
until 'we girls' left home

but we failed to be sisters who
shared   had secrets   schemed
promised   bargained   laughed

we were split down the middle
each to be there for one parent
no time to be daughters in the back
seat with our own careless dreams

There was a time when…

she could not remember a day that her sister
had not made her cry
no matter how hard she tried
to hold back the tears
before the day was over
it was a wet ruin like all the others

she had no way of understanding it
what might have been said, not said
how and when the hurt happened
it seemed like a mistake
and mistakes have
to be rectified

but the mistake had no shape
it just kept becoming more
if it looked like mending
it spread itself a little deeper
and sat in clotted corners
they were immuned

to the constant wounding
it never healed
no new skin was ever broken
no sharp incision was made
with beginning and end
no sound that made her jump

just a slow heat that crept to boiling
without alarm   warning   lifesaver
but she could now
she could rescue it
give it a form now
give it a name

she was ready
to leap from the cauldron
stop the slow dying
bury fear in the fathoms
fling open her heart
watch the trust creeping

into her lips
knowing her desire
could only speak healing
make words that came
from deep soul yearning
make way for their

ease and laughter

I believed

I was not the
kind of sister
she wanted to have

and although we tried
waiting   giggling
yelling   laughing

we had absorbed a
meanness we called
sisterly love

and the bruising – I
thought was joking
the battle of wills – I called pride

we learnt civility and caution
then silence and distance
then to be stubborn and safe

what do you do
with all that hidden
loyalty and hope

Footnote

last night I dreamt I stood
in my sister's shoes

they were worn
strange in shape on my foot

indented by her toes
sunk at the heel

marks so familiar
yet so utterly foreign

their warmth and smell
and softness

turned me
down side
up

Rare

in haste
to the rocks

and back
before

the tide takes
our footprints

at last
in step

Letters between us

on my side of the world
I woke with this summer prayer

open the nut shell
breathe in the
sweet nourishment

not for another minute be blind to

the renewing light
the joy of inner wisdom
sacred knowledge

feel the future dissolve

the strength of darkness
and not knowing
the courage of weakness and hopelessness

breathe in the

shadows
laws
limits

deeper and cleaner

until self is
one cloud upon
the hillside

And I read your morning paintings
from a wintery hemisphere

the waters are whispering
a soft mist filling

the sun still glancing
wild birds calling

a quiet tide rising
old wind sighing

ducks in formation
mother seal feeding

amber lamp glow
crackling fire wood

kind faces mirroring
voices so tender

japanese tub
last leaves falling

marmalade toast
ginger tea

all seems correct
you offer to me

I kiss your sweet letter
agree and agree   xx

Update

still in our house on water legs
gentle lapping without stopping
knowing it has a job to do

like everything else
the pouring rain
soaring seagulls

the slick redwood boards
and white teapot
the patient chair

all know their task

mine is to be with God
the wonder of sharing this space
with a soul who is fragile and kind

to be grateful and open
to the space that is offering
a new me

to surrender
to anchor
to journey

Dear sister

can you believe how
far we have come
become

it is so new and
yet already old
who

would have thought we
could bridge these
seven decades and more

of separation and foreignness
to discover pure ease
and sameness

it is a gift to our patience
and trust
and believing

it will be perfect to
see you come through
those Customs doors

and know we have days
to love and look after
and be so grateful

travel sweetly and
I'll be there

wondering why it had taken so long

Receiving

leaning into the chill of a
morning of pale blue
a pigeon balloons its
throat
and I'm filled
with new breath

*there are times when you need to
say thank you over and over again*

Four Birthing Days

You first made me mother

I didn't understand the
mightiness of your gift
I had no idea it would
keep cutting
such mysterious gems
polishing the purest
touch stones

fifty years of
watching a soul
unfolding
deepening and widening
its place on earth
witnessing ones blood
shape a destiny

a moon flower performance
every day

Be manifest

watching you grow into forty
has been like witnessing the
emerging of an island
already forested and fruited

Testament

turning thirty is biblical
there's a completion   an offering
a sacrifice   a celebration

how did you know all that

And you…

your warm porcelain
holiness
now wise marble

many moons

Their turn to sing

it's easy to sweep back in time
the sound of small feet tripping through my sleepy haze
they leap like notes of music filling every
pre-lined page
voices ebb and flow over sand castles, sailing boats, echo in
the gum leaves
hands offer cicada shells, lizard skin, stolen eggs
from secret trees

the moon brightens such sweet faces
captures the wrinkle on the nose, that curl
flicker of an eye lid, timid smile
the question on the trembling lips
touches a tiny body as it steps, struggles, skips
first words for favourite things
tears that well but can't overflow

I tell the moon the stories
now smiling patiently
it helps to sweep back in time
hold each – one by one
hear their whispering lullabies
now stroking me to sleep

Yuletide

every nose   nail
or knee
has a brush
of you and me

singing daughters
joking sons
serving laughter
by the tonnes

nine grand boys
clear-skinned faces
making prizes
naming places

baby girl being
passed and kissed
not a piece of her
is missed

careful gifts of
love and making
waiting for the
giving   taking

garden food
washed and ready
pizza oven hot
and steady

joy is served
peace is taken
in our grace
no one's forsaken

look at you
and you at me
such gratitude
for all we be

Once removed

through my grandmother
eyes I watched

as parents come in laden
from the car

dog and cat dart artfully
through forbidden door

children heave themselves free
of unwanted bags   books   boots

the house is cold and no one
wants to collect firewood

the clock strikes too close
to dinner time

and the space fills with
hungry tired energy

from nowhere mother serves
bowls of steaming food

and I think
life is a paradox

where mother seeds
move mountains

These unplanned gifts

atoms of vision and mystery
flashes of divine light
breath of yearning fire
love polished from my heart

Home splendour

the kitchen's full of music
there's a flurry as he chops finely
shakes a pan   folds cream

plates become paintings
crisp spinach leaves   garden-laid eggs
salmon from the market

he scatters orange nasturtiums
inky lobelia   freshly crushed
coriander   grinds fat peppercorns

breakfast kids   he calls around the house
across the garden
two nymphs fly through the door

dad   you're the best
it's so scrummy
so pretty

full of glorious restraint and vast

an abundance of endless worlds

On the golden floor

rugs carried home from camel rides
cushions made of desert thread
water lips azure glaze
ancient gong sings silently

incense ash amongst fallen petals
black Madonna catches light
beads an offering on the altar
candle floats in jasmine scent

I hear her chanting from a circle of sun

City coffee

he stood at the lights
directly opposite

tall and black-suited
long neck brown

white-starched
open

an ease in his elegant stride
as he stepped from the kerb

in the hand that swept his chest
to remove the security badge

he paused midstream as an
oncoming pedestrian rushed the lights

beckoning the
traffic to wait a bit longer

I watched as he came closer
to the window where I sat

with two glasses of water
gladdened and grateful

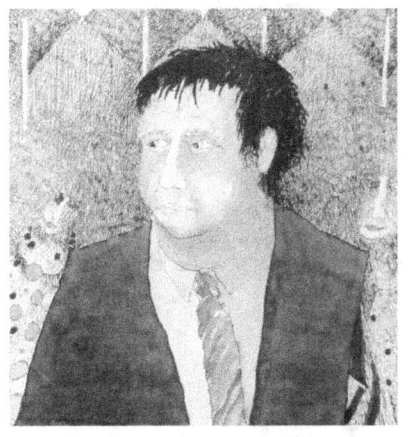

with the colossal safety of a full moon

rich as the great summer's yield

What an Eden she created

bush berry creepers climbers
fruit fragrance chaos colour
screeching flocks mountain rocks
slabs of slate chooks that wait
pizza oven boys' own coven

fires that gather smiling friends
verandas to salute the sun
honour the waxing waning moon
bushland clearings for yoga and prayers
doors wide open to music and song

night candles and twinkling lights
humming voices
tender food
socked feet and animal paws
incense curls in paradise

He

Like sandstone

Elegant   Building block
Open to carving
Used in fortifications
Castles   Cathedrals

Sedimentary   Consolidates   Clarifies
Easily penetrated
Changes shape with time
Bears imprint of wind   weather   water

Often employed as ballast
Withstands high velocity
Creates stability by settling
Used to engrave   clean or blast

Composed of sound grains
Strong   Edifice-malleable   Adaptable
A solid mass offering firm support
Needs protection against unwanted whittling

made of the most regular minerals
found on earth
giving it a huge impression around
the globe

She

soft and composed
a ribbon of welcome
unfurling quiet warmth
beauty and kindness

space filled with fervour
with rigor   intention
she's poised to hear
to know   to offer

amid music and flowers
vegies and fruit
clay gods and lanterns
bird feeders and shrines

feel her wide laughter
arms full of passion
brave heart of freedom
knowing no binds

find her with diamonds
rubies   black pearls
burnishing   gilding
silver and gold

watch her at night
in stillness and peace
mapping the day's voyage
with broad insight

at last see her offering
her breath and her body
as she prays and gives thanks
in still candle light

Him

If I could paint
he would be green

pine green
fresh   tall   dark

and brown
brown for making

strong square hands
drawing exquisite fine lines

carving   planning   inlaying
his intricate designs

there'd be a splash of navy blue
for legs astride the work bench

body still   meditative   focused
head bowed   wondering   resolving

then there's red for the host
and huge generosity

for the sharing and caring of others
the kindness and camaraderie

silver splashes his laughter
and his dances of delight

and purple for his bursting heart
passionate and vulnerable

the finest gold leaf
captures the glow of his love

like lacework

for everyone
and now for himself

Her

I'll try to describe her
she's golden and tanned
a smile of peace on her lips
belief in her hand

something exotic around her neck
a splash of colour in her hair
her legs are often in yoga pose
long arms strong usually bare

through bush and beach
and foreign lands
she carries a child
and others by hand

her heart full of
compassion and time
for friendships, shared
food, home-made wine

she paints and draws
prints and sews
explores and experiments
offers all she knows

women seek her at birthing time
soak up her ways with child
she shares it all thoughtfully
how to be mindful   how to run wild

looking into her faraway gaze
there is a fresh dream evolving there
an urge to discover new dimensions of self
remaining earthed   attuned   full of care

almighty mix

Sleepless

night melts like syrup
blacker and blacker molasses
stars burn   scorch
fall and fade

in beds and cribs sleepers sigh   cry
bound to the tireless dark
staring wide-eyed
pinned down

summoning foolish things
stupid lovely things
all their precious   unwise
past

and still they wish
they'd never stir
sleep like the dead
the bed a tomb

yet something amazing
can happen when
the world is asleep
without an idea of time or place

no sound
sensation
daily demands
no searching light

glued to my chair
silent
I remember all I ever
wanted to do was write

There are no shortcuts to peace of mind

just growing
that root
one more
day

into the dearest
freshest
deep down
grandeur

Just let yourself love what it loves

you are that self – not its judge
hear you announcing your place

as the sun moves and the rain clears
as soft animals settle and birds return

listen to what you love – calling you
into the family of things

A merciless instructor

each of them cross legged
with one foot resting on the floor
the other swaying or kicking the air
passing the time in stolen sun
a moment forgetful
of their morning deed

before he rounded the corridor
they'd unravelled their twists the reverie
landed full height
heels toes together
arms stock still
eyes glued to the clock tower

just seconds away from evening detention
weekend community service
once upon a time caning

consequences of
hands in pockets
fallen down socks

Passions

whether inflamed with zeal
or with the bitterness of pain
wild with delight
drowned in misery

imagine them as pots of paint
your brush quivering with rapture
stroking anything with miracles
highlighting hidden mystery

Almighty Mix

we can't be fully human without plunging
into mystery

can't thrive on grand schemes, smooth
principles, creeds, theories

the heart doesn't pulse with answers
understanding   manipulation

it plumps and purrs with unfathomable
faith   sacred intimacy

the marvellous   messy   soul in us
is a deep   wide   unboxable spirit

Grace

when we don't ask why or how
long for satisfaction
solutions

we are fed by
deep changes
guided to our fate

when we allow fantasy
reverie
ride the unpredictable

sit in wonder at the
turning points
and tumbling

shifting view point
chaos
holy nothingness

we are....

We know art

through line and form
making and marking
word and gesture
colour and sound
pirouettes

each speaks of the
inner workings
of creation
seeks to unfold the
harmony of life

takes us to our
own reflection

The great difficulties

that someone will feel his
lack of attention

the trying too hard
the fear of foolishness

will learn not to come again
not to wait

will caste his future
mute the past

is sure to examine
his sameness   strangeness

will misjudge his belief
his aim   his honour

undo his certainty
his very reason

and for them he'll become
something so other

It's easy to fear

our own strength without knowing
stop short of the marvellous

not lunge into that last leap
stay small for others

what suffering
rejection

ridicule
blame

matters…

when we are diving
into magnificence

No room at the...

we drove through rows of bare hungry houses
no one allowed to breathe in life

the world writhes with wandering homeless
we dare not let them in to light candles

rounding the corner a fairy-lit tree sparkled
through a drapeless window

in the empty room a child threaded
tinsel through coloured biscuits

there was room at the inn
for life to be born

some wordy master
at last unlocked the waste
undid the suffering
and let the Light in

Christ Mas

I dreamed

of green feathered
breasts
crimson with blood
or was it the
falling sun

they move through the moments

Of babies

in the lamplight downy hair
shone like warm oil

his breath filled the bowl
warm as bedtime milk

wide spread eyes opened
and closed soft as a moth

mother's love emptied into
the honey hollow of a new heart

an armful of quiet
in your father's arms
simply getting on
with sleeping

today you swung so high
I thought our laughter
would never bring
you down

Hatti's noticing

I often find
after gazing in
your eyes
all others
look faulty

tiny as you are
you straightened
your cup cake knees
leaned into his face
and sang with
your grandfather

another dawn
and your eyes
filled the room
with such a sparkle
the air stopped
to catch breath

content that all
was well
you tucked the muslin
beneath you nose
stroked a downy ear
and found sleep
again

Morning glory with my granddaughter

wake up   wake up
I promise I've put the kettle on

hurry   hurry   cause night's gone
you know what that means

we watch the darkness rise from the sand
a dragon claws its way from sea – shadow

water nymphs sprinkle ocean mist
a dancer saddles a sea horse

gulls shake their neck bells
fish pull in a new tide

when the darkness finishes
we have to beat the sun home

otherwise the chickens
won't lay our breakfast

Tender perspective

I had him scurrying the rivulet
searching for an escaped scarf

it's my favourite I insisted
surely I'll find it   just one more look

but Hatti   it's not like
some one has died

he caught my breath and I hoped
someone else was delighting in it

......

Wrapped in awe of such
warm porcelain holiness
new sibling reminds me ..
if she would stop breathing she
would be my favourite doll

......

And then they sprint

long-limbed leopard
muscling a nose ahead
to the finishing line
whilst the other
runs like tumbleweed
more in the air than on ground

Too fast to youth

from porcelain perfect
absorbing and melting
trusting and believing

now hungry to discuss
argue
hammer out possible answers

all teeth and hair and hope
with their purple clothes
and blinding beanies

wild as the sun
boiling in the sea
sleepy as waterlogged sponges

they move through the moments
like a band of Hell's Angels
still my gang of heaven-dropped blessings

Moment of decision

he wondered if he continually changed the
expression on his face would
there be no time for the wrong one

within minutes he stepped from the kerb of anxiety into a
wide street of comfy certainty

Leading me on

we all change the world
for being here
our ways and our timing

but instead of my past
and the faith that has
fired me to be and do

I notice it's my offspring
who sculpt and script me
to leave a better place for my coming

Holiday boys

eyes glancing…

flashing with laughter   wild in glee
kicking and catching
deliciously free

into the surf to take a wave
waiting on boards
silent and brave

hanging their rods
in pale moonlight
perfect spot for squid to bite

strumming guitars and throaty song
they harmonise
and cruise along

out of the blue
all is still
like babies who have had their fill

These Tender Teenagers

without shadow or cloud

Time for term

they fell through
the door

sighing   tangled
wind burnt

from spinning waves
and flying sand dunes

quick to recognise the
end of cloud-watched days

they stacked salt-stained play
sea-licked laughter

into closets of summer memories
and readied their taut strong bodies

for tomorrow's
grey green uniform

Cymbals

when a thunderstorm
gathers up the Derwent

spewing weed and silt and debris
we watch it as we do our grandson on percussion

there are flashes of fury and icy flow
loose vibrations and lightning bolts

we see him straight as the rough barked oak
his drum sticks stirring white water on the cliffs

feet making wavelets or roaring surges
his head nodding to inner tides

hair a floating mass of sun lit weed
the world lost to his lidded eyes

No longer boy-shaped

filled for year upon year
with darting daring
and curiosity

now our grandchildren
graceful forms of
ease and concern

move midst
the world
like sliding water over stone

Music festival

they danced as on hot coals
sang till they hurt
made music   made friends
loved their naked skin

barely making the tent for sleep
collapsing under a wet sky
felt the wind the fallen cloud
the short black night

light-shot dawn cracked them open
like mountain springs
spread-eagled feet balanced   poised
felt the new morning rhythm

breakfast of sound and pulse

Summer work

they spill into construction sites
waiting on tables
picking summer berries
scrubbing café potatoes

hammers   ladders
hard hats
wide brims   harvest baskets
fingernails of earth and gratings

aproned
black shod
white cuffs
hair tied   hand behind

all practice for
soon to be gone
left home
moved beyond

words to a grandmother called Hatti

Such grand kinder conversations

Thank you for the book
I love it
I read it with
my whole mouth

If the world
was really good
I would be
the sun
and you
the moon
and we
would meet
for breakfast
in a different
country
every morning

Fairies just know
one left me
something
this morning
even before
I asked
for it

Whoever slices
the moon
all the time
and keeps making
you so old
mustn't be very nice

It was one of those times
when evening was all
afternoon
'noon-on' a grandson
named it
because nothing in the sky
tells you its now something else

What do you think, Hatti

loving someone
and being loved
can't feel the same
can they

because you can't feel
how someone
feels when you
love them

except they both
feel like being
tucked up on a
lightening night

You know why you're so wobbly now?

because your roots
aren't travelling
downwards
they're going sideways
dig in deeper   Hatti

A new kid came today
and he had spots all
over his face
like stars in the
milky way

When I'm grown
there won't be
anything dad
can do that
I can't do
maybe I can do
what he
can't do

We're not really
going anywhere, Hatti
it's all forever
like inside a dream

nothing makes sense
when you wake up
everything's on top
of one another

Don't you love
watching the clouds
paint the earth

it's like the artist
keeps changing
his mind

moving the shapes
till the pattern's
right

Often, Hatti, when I sleep on the grass
I can hear everything
the birds thieving ripe fruit
ants marching dead flies
clouds puffing guessing games
bees in bumbledom
even the walnuts dangling
does that mean I'm asleep
or truly awake

Sometimes my brother looks
like a night sky
sprung with planets and
a flying saucer

My brother is a shooting star
hurtling through the air
landing here
landing there

I wish he'd stay next to the moon
and we'd just skype each other

We went to wonderland
today in the bush everything had shrunk
as though eaten by Alice
and the picnic looked like Hatti
was having a mad tea party

I think a very tidy witch
must have shaken the leaves
and swept the grass
because the trees are empty
and there's no mess
who else would have
such long strong arms
and a fast   clever broom

School Camp and Australia Rules

I'll be spotlighting, Hatti
We'll catch each other
with our torches
You have to drop when you're
beamed

How I'd love to see such fallen stars

Collingwood pies
Go, The Magpies
The best
Because they sing when they want
Flick their tails
Catch mid air
Land wherever is right
They're half bird
That's why they win

Cats now

why do you love cats best now
they don't make me feel bad
when I don't worry about them

I'm tired of not caring enough for dogs
does that mean I don't love them
I wish they knew I did. I'm just tired even
though I'm not old

games with grand and god children

I thought of what I was, Hatti

and mostly I'm a monkey
I watch from the tree tops

swing and loop and
spy and notice

invite and entice
and trick and tempt

and climb high
when I've caused havoc

BUT I just learnt that
I was born in the year of the monkey

and the sign is good
I'm funny and playful

witty   intelligent   agile
loyal   talkative   work hard

and I'm competitive
I like that

it helped me win my medal
it makes me feel brave and ready

I'm glad I was born in 2004
and guess what?   2018 is the Year of the Monkey

You must be a goat

because everything you have
you love to give away
goats do that

they give their milk and meat
and hair and skin
give things people make and use

their skin can be parchment.
that's like you
making paper for your letters and poems

even pencils
you made them from their horns
and their bones could be

knitting needles or
you'd make chop sticks for us
or maybe an arrow

or you turned a little toe into a brooch
once you plaited a goat's beard hair
hanging it from your key ring

and they must have
eyes at the back of
their head like you

and they eat like you
nibbling and browsing
all the time

they're not fussy
except when they really like
something they eat lots

and they walk and climb
and balance and escape
get to the top and feel free

yell out to the other goats and
cuddle up with their young
and buck or charge an intruder

and they call their offspring
KIDS

I wrote about a camel
because I saw one at Uluru
it was my best story
here it is for you, Hatti

camel-coloured
its carved humps like cliff tops
against the sky
eyes deep hollows searching the horizon

slowly the boney strong
body settled every muscle
before lowering its
front legs to the sand

knees firmly anchored
the large head checked
the vast distance and began
the beautiful movement

of lowering the ancient shape
till it rested like a sphinx
on the hot desert earth

Hope you like it
xx

Hatti, you asked me to write about an animal.

I did. I wrote about the goats
we saw at Byron Bay

The breeze played in the strong hair of his beard his horns
were ready to butt and lock or push his way through bush
and overhanging beach briars

he dug his hoofs into the shaley rock and
mounted the most protruding edge
pushing himself to the furtherest of things

balanced on the cliff face staring out to sea
he needed to be alone, just him between the swirling sea and
windswept sky

below was his herd waiting for him
waiting to run wild as a mob until they
curled up closely that night – safe yet free
Capricorns like me!

I want to be a cow
slow and calm and kind
with hips like down-filled sofas

the farmer will milk me on bended knee
and put me on to dew-wet grass
to rock and chew and gaze

I don't speak or worry or roam
or know about fees or phones and loans
the hardships of cities or loaded freighters

heavy with sweet milk
safe among my black   white herd
standing ground in drought and storm

I'm grateful to be weathered and worn
as that is what I came to be
a cow – living it all quite naturally

Lotsa love,
Your God daughter
xx

I am a camel

humpy and lumpy
walking without
water
recycling my food

pushing through limits
sitting   resisting
refusing
stubborn
determined

I'd live or die for you
believe
have faith in
go down on
my knees for you

sail you through the desert

how's that for poetry, Hats?

Dearest,
you are also an ox
born that zodiac year

makes you patient   dependable
hard-working   fair-minded   kind

trust worthy   certain   responsible
and guess what? you love purple and pink

Of course, I'm a rat

I'm curious cautious clever
flexible tricky alert
affectionate quick tidy

I have a great memory
grasp new skills
and make good friends

soon I'll be ten
and rats get better and
better at everything they do

Golden dragons
born 2000

there are three of us
we are legendary
our power strength good luck

smart honest caring
we are fired with love
for nature challenge imagination

like all magnificent dragons we must be
bold unconstrained determined
live by our own rules and flare when it matters

lucky we are three
we put each other's fire out
when it's time for the cave

Curious

I'm wondering, Hatti

jealousy – an attack on difference
or greed for the same

in trying so hard
can we become harder

in my busyness
do I mind my own business

you always get me thinking
and I need another talk about
maybe nothing is there if
no one is looking at it

that's a tricky one, isn't it, dear one
I don't know if the soap stays drying
on the shell if we're not watching
or the chair doesn't wait
who knows what towels do
when there is no wet skin

let's talk soon

This tribe that is ours

their beauty enters
the nervous system
touches the soul
rests on the heart
serves every cell

these are the
tastes
smells
texture
that will feed me
as the present
dissolves

who but me
will remember
what it feels like
to have held
everyone of these
within hours
of their arrival

Scarce words

like deep harmony

can keep in time
with our breath

nothing said
in vain

white daisies hardly breathe at all

magpies sit in singing silence

a creamy sky scoops the day

as a dusk plover folds her young

their breath swells travels surges

Grandfather's Birthday

as stars arrive to a waiting sky
they take up their allotted spot
reflecting and rippling the tribal pool
of genes   gestures   repeated   refined

like musicians in their orchestral place
strumming and tuning   finding the pitch
they balance and ready
for the nod to perform

a wave gathering on the horizon
their breath swells   travels   surges
spilling the shores with their laughter
the air with birthday song

and he becomes three score and ten

My aunt

advised me strongly
on her dying bed
not to worry if I sometimes
forgot her   didn't think of
her for years
just remember when you do
I asked you to smile
laugh out loud
even swear a little
so that I remember who I was
she giggled

On a son becoming fifty

sweet fruit has ripened
from hidden seed
and tender flame

from a landscape of
love and labour
from belief and
from trust

this day is a harvest
a reaping and gathering
a celebrating   jubilating
shouting with joy

it's a thanksgiving
an acknowledgement
an arrival   a triumph

of the life that you took
and grew with such passion

for the journey you've walked
so lush   so luminous
brave   believing

No wonder

in his last moments
my father knew to thank
one more time
the wonder of it all

the final tragedy
must be
the voice that
mumbles…

at the end of the day
it is no more
than an egg timer
a street sale

mindless of
the beauty
the mystery
that got us here

After glow

although my father
has been dead
nearly thirty years

people still say
whether they knew
or not

him or me
when
he was alive

that a light passes
over my face
when I
speak of him

11 November 2017

Remembrance Day, my father's birthday

I saw my father today
I saw his chiselled face
his faded eyes
set mouth
shock of white hair

I knew his resignation
determination
loyalty
steadfastness
the guarantees he kept

I felt my father today
his love
his protection
his strength
his sacrifice for us

I remembered his sadness today
the grief of a tortured heart
broken dreams
promises
the loss of faith

when I looked again
he was shining
peace-filled
no longer a returned soldier
more an archangel

Why Joy Hope, my mother?

love without Joy
is like breath
without air

life without Hope
a ridiculous
care

declared my grandmother
as she explained the naming
of her third daughter

whilst we sat in facing chairs
she making balls of wool
from my outstretched arms

and there is your aunt Grace
and Faith and Verity, too
I wanted to call your uncle

Valour

she whispered
through
nearly tears

Beyond

perhaps there will be a great grandchild
who is the door   the opening
to letting in   letting out

allowing me to be
sunlight on a stream
fire flame in the dark

a pulse   a breath   a dream
prayer rain   sun-filled silence
just one more time

my mother whispered having
wondered how long it might
take for no one to remember her

she'll live on in the blue hydrangeas

Whose Song

against a purple mountain a wide bay surges
white waves lick golden beaches back to rock
full full moon drags the tide across the sky
delivering virgin sand for new-day walkers

in tights and boots woolly coat and scarf
I step out and into the pink-mauve morning
like an English midwife in midwinter
striding towards my next miracle

along the beach flotsam is strewn
not in wavering lines left by the last wave
but in heaps spaced irregularly where a sea monster may have
heaved and spewed

blue plastic and cuttlefish   pink weed
shining lid   a bramble still with flower   punctured ball
green sandal   ice cream tub
an army of milk bottle rings

mottled oak leaf   pine cone
rosy bottle brush   fat gum nuts
perfume the wet wind has
plucked from lemon grass

I sing as I climb the dunes trying to rhyme my words   I'm
singing for raw souls   singing-in another day   singing that
they feel the strength of black oaks   the splendour of cliff heat

I sing about a clay pitcher that is never full – leaving space for
trust   about the empty fountain that the sun can dry clean
the wild wind that carries flower seed to waiting lands

and the shadows where only black jasmine grows
a song about the homeland being in our heart
and our peace in the garden beneath blossoming beans

our joy can be like honeybees feeding as we tremble   and our
sadness a lone moon believing in the sun
I sing to notice something else has already come

A woman I know

she is a mid-life wife   mother of sons
a story of tasks and play and making
of caring   sharing   wondering

and embarking on a pilgrimage

the pilgrim journey is a song line
a travelling to a sacred place
covering the distance is an act of devotion

there is a number of certain holy things to do

to begin a pilgrimage we must be prepared to
step out of the ordinary   the safe   the predictable
let go of the familiar   the kindness and comfort

trust in an inexplicable   exquisite knowing

we are seeking transformation and
need to create fresh space for the conversion
close our eyes   deeply breathe

take our first step into the wilderness

there is a particular way to travel
the ritual walking is an ancient act
a chance to connect with our wholly selves

with holy other

it is more than a tracing of geography
it is a landscape of questions and insights
of invitations   suggestions   guidance

the nature of the destination can fade

we lay ourselves open to the kindness of sun
the comfort of tree trunk   the safety of silence
to the extraordinary   the foreign   the unknown

to the dreams creation has for us

we embarked on our journey with precision
and planning   with weighing of options
and fast forwarding of outcomes

holding onto the ache for faith and for freedom

every footfall we step out of ourselves
out of the narrow pathways within
beyond the chasms of fear and control

to encounter the grace and love that dwell within
to live to the music   the song
the dance of spirit

that lie in the valley of emptiness

If life is a leaf

that seasons tear off
they will bind again
with fresh new green

to shapes beyond

There are times when we outlive our host

the single grain formed from irritant
grows a pearl as lustrous as deep sea

and offers itself to a hand that will take
it on to shapes beyond the scalloped shell

Another turning

will I remember its sweetness
kissed hurrying grand boys before school
wandered home to fill the house with daisies
smell of baking muffins
Gregorian chants

made a brew of sympathy with a tear-stained friend
felt my mother in the shining tea pot
wished I could tell her how much I loved
polishing silver

content and complete with letter posting
sea breeze played with my skirt
puffed at my hair as I rounded the hills
heavy with perfume of jasmine
magnolias of waxed wine

I sighed at my day's simplicity
hourless
unmeasured
need I remember what age I turned

Time has stolen much

blanched my hair
pencilled my skin

paled my eyes and
dulled my ears

it's left me feeling

like a sun filled vase
a moon lit garden

the white-horse ocean
wild mountain air

and still time for

pink faded petals
a twilight-blue shadow

There is less of me

as I absent myself

more part of cosmic creation
the living earth

make more space
for the God within

gently curving
carving change

Transition

when all is packed away
most likely never opened again
memories allowed for no reason at all

there can be a thrill in stepping
into nothingness
eyes wide shut

At 3 a.m.

just the ticking of the clock
and me beside you
waiting for your next breath

Ephemeral

night fuses with
day
gossamer spins
dawn

light blanches
stars
windows bear
offerings

dreams mere
question marks
hope dares to
creep

Some are in haste to say goodbye

don't seem to want to take note of
all that has been
all that is

some linger longer to say farewell
dispense   detach   distance
make time for others to receive

we may need to wait
allow for the time between
ending and leaving

Now this age

we permit anger
don't need approval
or to be understood

we are easy
fellow travellers
letting go our luggage

without a ticket
a platform
a map

we dance in the don't-know
on a road of
radical mystery

Wild bereavement

you can't do that…

…leave me here in the emptiness
even a cat knows to climb the walls
rub up against the furniture

nothing seems different
but nothing is the same
nothing has moved

but there's more space
no one lights
the lamp by your chair

there's no other set of footsteps
on the staircase
no tea in your cup

something's not starting at its usual time
something doesn't happen as it should
someone was always, always here

then suddenly disappeared
stayed disappeared
refuses to be found

if you can do that
so can I
just help me disappear
to you

Changes

this evening feeling the wind on my skin
and noticing the exquisite difference it made
I wonder what it becomes
having been felt

and of course I ask the night
how strange will it be
for the last one left
and no one to share the difference

then I notice the moon
enlightens the trees
leaves are wet with delight
a flute speaks of love
lavender perfumes as I pass
deep emerald fills the sky

always

Several things inspired putting such a collection together –

anniversaries
beginnings and ends
children's clarity

This year Bruce and I celebrate
fifty-two years of marriage

in the sky is a star ruby
passion   protection
prosperity
beside is a star of eternity
deep love and gratitude

My sister and I healed a long period
of confused estrangement

we let difference alienate us
now we smile at each
other's unique way of decorating
declaring   decoding

It is nearly thirty years since our father died
soon twenty years since the death of our mother

we all surprise each other
how often we say
wish they were at this table
right now

Our children are all mid-life
their children leaving home

we shuffle on the branches
making room
filling gaps

But the most urgent call
for this book came from
grandchildren

What will you do with all this, Hatti?
You have to put it all into a book
Everything
Everything on the floor here
Just like it is
And that means everything we have written too

And so I dared
and I gift it
back to them

www.ingramcontent.com/pod-product-compliance
Lightning Source LLC
Chambersburg PA
CBHW070100120526
44589CB00033B/815